THE ANCIENT RUINS OF SEDONA

photos by
TOM JOHNSON

text by
HOYT JOHNSON

Today, much is written and said about how people recently have discovered the amenities of Sedona, as though its spectacular red rocks, fertile land, splashing creeks, abundant sunshine and mild climate were something new. In fact, the magnificent richness of this land was enjoyed by Native Americans centuries ago, of course — and its unique pleasures caused them to build impressive homes on spectacular sites that often pale the choices made by modern discoverers.

Obviously, it's not fair to compare; yesterday was then and today is now.

Nonetheless, restrictions imposed by considerations such as food, water and protection were just as limiting to these Native Americans as zoning ordinances, building permits and architectural guidelines are to this age's inhabitants.

Evidence suggests that the choices made more than 700 years ago were wise and artful, indeed.

Palatki, one of the largest cliff dwellings in the Sedona area, is beautiful at any time — at sunset it is spectacular!

The vast Verde Valley was born of earthly uplifts, faulting that produced broad zones of fractured rock and erosion caused by retreating seas millions of years ago. These forces produced a verdant river basin that directed the evolution of this unique area's historic development.

Reaching from the Mogollon Rim — which marks the southern boundary of the Colorado Plateau — to the Black Hills, the area identified as the Verde Valley includes the creek-rich, red-rock canyons of Sedona and the surrounding land.

Just as water, lush vegetation and plenteous wildlife attract visitors today, numerous Native American cultures were drawn to this beautiful area centuries ago. The history of these early Native Americans extends over a period of approximately 1,400 years, starting in A.D. 1 and ending, mysteriously, about A.D. 1425.

Though the interpretation and chronological classification of what occurred during this historic period often is altered, or even discarded because of new evidence, it generally is conceded that the ancient cliff dwellings found in the Sedona area were constructed during The Honanki Phase, A.D. 1130-1300, when an influx of Sinagua increased the population in this red-rock region.

A substantial number of archaeologists attribute the introduction of an architectural style employing masonry construction to the Sinagua.

Some of this area's best-preserved ruins are located in remote sites that are very difficult to find and to get to. The correlation is obvious!

Petroglyphs are wonderful examples of prehistoric communication and documentation that today, are appreciated as beautiful, creative art.

Archaeologists credit the Sinagua with the development of masonry construction, an architectural style that was complemented by the use of the Sedona area's beautiful red rocks.

As with so many of Sedona's attractive features, the two largest cliff dwellings in this intriguing red-rock area have been labeled "world class" by learned authorities. These ancient ruins, named Palatki and Honanki, probably were occupied by Sinagua people between A.D. 1130 and A.D. 1280. Justification for assessing this time frame is based on a date determined by examining potsherds and the tree rings of wooden lintels, used for support over a door or window.

Apparently, the theory crediting the construction of these handsome dwellings to Sinagua who emigrated from the Flagstaff area is endorsed by the majority of archaeologists; others, however, relate the occupation of Sedona's canyons to a climate that was exceptionally warm and moist, thus attracting members of the Southern Sinagua culture who already were inhabitants of the Verde Valley.

Palatki and Honanki first were reported by Dr. Jesse Walter Fewkes of the Smithsonian Institute in 1895. Later, in 1911, Fewkes conducted test excavations at these sites while investigating Hopi migration. It was this early archaeologist who named these ruins Palatki and Honanki, Hopi words that mean "Red House" and "Bear House," respectively.

Palatki is composed of two separated pueblos, which suggests that two families lived here. Supporting this theory are circular, shieldlike pictographs that some archaeologists contend are clan symbols. The eastern pueblo, which is the largest, shows evidence of population growth by the addition of two rooms. The western pueblo features a kiva, or meeting room, indicated by the presence of a raised bench.

Originally, Honanki had as many as 60 rooms and a very large collection of pictographs. Unfortunately, many of these rooms and pictographs have been destroyed by pothunters, vandals and the aging process imposed by time. Nonetheless, the mysterious aura pervading Honanki is thick with excitement, causing challenging speculation.

Officials at the Sedona Ranger District are charged with stewardship of the Palatki and Honanki ruins, which are extremely popular curiosities for area visitors. This assignment requires the careful blending of contrasting interests; that is, these officials are faced with preserving the scientific value of these important sites, and at the same time, making them available for public enjoyment — not always an easy task.

Marietta Davenport, archaeologist at the Sedona Ranger District, is extremely adamant regarding respect for public lands: "Taking things from an ancient ruin is like tearing pages out of an exciting 'whodunit' — near the back of the book, no less. Even getting things out of order is like mixing up pages," she says. "What fun is it to read almost an entire mystery and then discover that important clues are missing?"

Obviously, the protection of ancient ruins is a very important matter. In that regard, the Sedona Ranger District's message is simple: "Don't change anything, don't take anything and don't leave anything!"

Davenport puts it another way: "People don't go into an art museum, approach a precious van Gogh painting and break off a little piece," she states.

Think about it!

Honanki, called a "world-class" dwelling, originally had as many as 60 rooms.

Though extremely beautiful, some sites obviously were chosen for the protective features of their almost-inaccessible locations.

Circular pictographs like those drawn on high, rock walls above Palatki are thought to be family, or clan, symbols.

Sedona's ancient ruins probably were occupied by Sinagua people between A.D. 1130 and A.D. 1280, a time frame determined by examining wooden lintels used as supports for doors, windows and roofs.

Respected author Donald E. Weaver Jr., writing in *Plateau* magazine, which is published by the Museum of Northern Arizona, describes rock art as "a categorical term that includes purposeful human modification of in-place rock surfaces by pecking, scratching, incising, engraving, drilling, carving, grinding and painting to produce preconceived images."

Weaver doesn't leave out much!

An important point this writer makes is that this art form only relates to *in-place* rock surfaces. "Thus, the bedrock grinding surfaces that result from grinding activities to produce seed flour are not considered rock art," he states.

So-called rock art exists in two basic forms, petroglyphs and pictographs, and the difference essentially is the same as what separates carving from drawing. Remember how the names of these forms were derived, don't mix them up, be able to explain their distinction and you'll be in a class almost by yourself. Probably, no other two terms are confused more often.

Petro and glyph, from the Greek prefixes "petra" and "glyphe," mean rock and carving, respectively. Picto, from the Latin prefix "pictus," when added to graph, means: pictured object used to convey an idea or information. Thus, carvings and peckings on in-place rocks are called petroglyphs, and drawings on these same surfaces are called pictographs.

In "Images on Stone," Weaver reports that pictographs are common in eastern Utah, the Grand Canyon, Canyon de Chelly and the Sedona area," but are uncommon or rare elsewhere." Once again, Sedona is fortunately endowed!

Imagine the appeal of sites such as this one, where the Sinagua lived, as compared to the flat, high plateaus to the north and the hot desert to the south. And so it always has been with Sedona!

Visiting an ancient Sinagua ruin is somewhat like entering a church; there is a reverence that commands silence. People talk softly and walk slowly, as they might if they were interrupting a worship service. Respect for what was accomplished so many centuries ago is a strong force that restrains normal exuberance, and often, this solemn mood causes visitors to view these magnificent ruins as if they *always* had been ruins. An almost-sacred respect inhibits the imagination of most visitors.

I suggest letting your mind have fun!

Imagine, if you will, that it is 700 years ago; recognize that the native people who lived at Palatki, Honanki and the other beautiful sites occupied at this time were humans filled with emotion, and that they experienced everyday joys and sorrows just as we do.

Flick a switch in your ear and hear the sound of people; push a button in your eye and see what they are doing. Whoops, step back a bit so the kids who are running around have room for their games.

Isn't it interesting to see people working in the irrigated fields far below where you are standing? Notice the women who are grinding corn over by the storage room. Hear their rhythmic motions?

Suddenly, a Sinagua mother shouts, "Don't go so close to the edge. I'm afraid you might fall!" A lookout on top of a red-rock pinnacle hollers, "Here comes George. He's on his way back from the river." Behind you, young women are admiring the work of an aging potter, and above you, a recognized artist is carving unique petroglyphs into the massive rock wall that protects this busy community.

What is readily apparent is that these people are enjoying specific tasks; it is obvious that they possess special skills and happily accept particular responsibilities. Near the kiva at the far end of this extensive pueblo, a serious, older gentleman — there is no doubt that he is a community leader — is welcoming other elderly residents to a meeting. Nearby, several women are weaving baskets — and just beyond, a soft-spoken man wearing more than the usual number of bracelets, necklaces and colorful strings of beads is counseling a woman who is holding a baby. Is he a doctor?

A burst of loud laughter and fast talking attracts your attention and you notice a gang of happy, teen-age girls waving clumps of brightly colored grasses that resemble pompons. It must be Friday, because these girls, who are jumping up and down and yelling, are inviting people to a special event. "Come over to the ball court," they say. "It's Palatki vs. Honanki today!"

"This pueblo is a busy place, full of life," you say with amazement. It is exciting to experience this glimpse of history in the making, and when your switch and button are turned off, you realize that a marvelous transformation has occurred: These enchanting ruins do not appear as mausoleums; in fact, the native people still are faintly visible, and your enjoyment has been enhanced tenfold.

You have, indeed, visited the Sinagua!

Published by
Sedona Publishing Company, 271 Van Deren Road, Sedona, AZ 86336

©1996 and 1993 by Sedona Publishing Company

Reproduction of material in whole or part
without permission is prohibited.

Printed by
Land O' Sun Printers, Scottsdale, AZ